The ascent of the common man of India

I am thankful for the cover art gift for the book. The cover art is of a child labor in India, clicked by an accomplished photographer Logan Hunt, a Tennessee based Indophile.

I am glad to have few supporting people with me through the thick and thin of my life. This book or for that matter most of what I have achieved in my life, would not have been possible without them, especially my mother and father. I am thankful to several magazines, blogs, and newspapers that have published my writings on socioeconomic issues. The chapters have been published individually before in various news sources. I have modified my original articles to fit the structure of the book.

Table of Contents

Prologue

This book is not a continuous flow of issues concerning India but a snapshot of few issues that I have focused on over the years, when I was spending lot of my energy on India's development. The suggestions presented are by no means exhaustive but an attempt to initiate dialogue and action by people interested in sustainable development of India. My own involvement with India is now from a perspective of how my scientific abilities can help development of large portion of humanity residing in this country, just as I would be delighted to be of use to any other place. From 2003 to one year after my return to India from United States, until 2015, I was committed to working from India, no matter what the situation and the perspectives were different. Bitter India experiences, realization that I can be more of use even for India from outside India and the last straw of witnessing joke of Indian academia over last two years have changed my perspective. Now my presence in India is not based on immutable principles but on temporary suitability and my concern with political wrangling has become close to zero. This second edition partially reflects my changed perspective, where focus is only on development but not on sociopolitical dynamics, which was an equal concern until some time back.

My past socioeconomic work has largely been focused on two regions: South Asia, a region of my birth and North America, a land of freethinkers that I fell in love with. Off late, I have been focusing on global issues but as I mentioned above that was not the case a few years ago, when somehow, despite series of horrible experiences, I could not cut the umbilical chord from India.

Before coming to India from USA in 2014, when most of the book was penned (original 17 chapters in 1st edition to now 7 abridged chapters in 2016), I used to think that it is the material conditions or few identifiable bottlenecks that prevent India's growth. I was under the delusion that when educated people are presented with solutions, they would act. They might disagree but it would be start of a dialogue that would eventually lead to action. I underestimated the bankruptcy of culture and mountain of apathy. I now realize whatever success Gandhi had against British was because British had to at least act British on face – maintain a semblance of morality. Had Gandhi faced Indians, he would have been dead, without much outcome. Now I laugh looking back at my naiveté about my approach to India. Compared to my original articles and the 2014 edition of the book, when I saw hope in one new political party AAP, which was spearheading anti-corruption drive, as a possible antidote to the old left, militant and separatist leftist forces, corrupt and dynastic Congress, sectarian politics of caste, minority separatism, regionalism, and the Hindu majority extremism of BJP, I now see no political party being knit from a different fabric than another. In this edition I have taken out chapters, which were focused on supporting AAP or criticizing other groups, to appropriately reflect my changed perspective that focuses less on politics but more on science, technology, and education to find solutions. The hope is that my book would initiate a dialogue.

My own life has taken a different course now, having had the wisdom to walk away. Instead of pointing out problems with hopes of a political change or hoping for someone else to do research to solve problems, I now run a data science effort (www.dataisnotjustdata.com), which focuses on sustainable development in addition to doing commercial projects. Earlier my life used to be divided between biological science research, art, literature, social activism, and some personal time. Now social activism is replaced by much more satisfying data-science, where I focus on issues of development without being concerned much with national boundaries or political players running the affairs. I find myself of lot more use to this planet, where I can use my technical knowledge and creativity to solve problems instead of arousing people in hope that they would solve problems. I hope you find my suggestions on sustainable development useful for India or for any other country, where they might be relevant. After all there is only one planet currently inhabitable for humans.

Chapter 1. North East India: A paradise unexplored or a paradise lost?

North East India represents seven percent of Indian area and 3.7% of Indian population. These figures hide the immense diversity of languages, ethnicity, culture and biodiversity as well as the wealth of natural resources. With pockets that are relatively untarnished with human exploitation, unlike most of the India, this place offers a cleaner slate than rest of the country to write a new story of a sustainable development. The perils on the road to grand promise of this place arise from several unresolved issues of history. Depending on what people define as the epicenter of a parochial monolithic cultural identity: Lahore, Delhi, Patna, Thiruvananthapuram or Kolkata, one might find North East India further apart than say Indonesia. North East India and for that matter, several troubled regions of India, can only become full participants to the Indian story, only, when Indians understand that unlike several more monolithic countries, India had a different history of national evolution. India is not a manifestation of expansion of city-states on ethnic or linguistic lines. For Europeans until Renascences, Hindustan used to be area around Indus and everything to the east of it including South Asia and Parts of South East Asia. In contrast, for majority of Indians (and not all), their country used to be whatever small territories inhabited by people alike them. Even a place hundred miles away could be pardes (foreign country).

With national identities still evolving constructs, for NE to be a full participant in the Indian story, India needs to study the following problems:

1) Current underdevelopment of its border regions, effecting NE, with majority of the agricultural sector being involved in subsistence farming and at times only one highway running through rather large regions.

2) Recent demographic shifts add to sources of conflicts. There are several examples of both incidental and state encouraged demographic shifts in the region. The incorporation of Sikkim by India, which was a separate country until 1975, only happened after Nepalese migrants became the majority in the state. In Tripura, influx of Bengali people has rendered the majority Tripuri people to be now just 30% of the population. Development, in my opinion, would be contingent on ethnic harmony and not arousing ethnic strife.

3) What most Indians don't know is that India was first populated by groups of human waves that are classified by anthropologists as Austroloid and Mongoloid, both the predominant groups in Northeast. It is ethnically one of the most diverse regions of India. This diversity at times manifests in the form of tribal rivalries. Cultural differences of neighbors can range from nuanced differences to as big of differences as being a patriarchal or a matriarchal society. There are several autonomous state demands in the region that if smartly dealt with, can ease ethnic strife.

4) The hypocrisy of several Indians claiming Northeast as integral to India, when there is trouble with neighboring countries over border and immigrants, while forgetting it at the times of peace is hurting region's full integration. This mistreatment

extends to treatment of Northeast people as second grade citizens in mainland India. A fair treatment is needed.

5) Heavy handed and indiscriminate response by Indian armed forces and continuation of Armed Forces Special Provisions Act (AFSPA) are sources of ongoing resentment. Northeast has witnessed the only bombing of India's territory by Indian Air Force. Po Zoramthanga who went on to become the chief minister of Mizoram, once said that the main reason he joined separatist Mizo National Front was because of "Relentless bombing of Aigawi in 1966". Nagaland has several veteran citizens who claim alive skinning of their comrades in the Naga Nationalist movement by Indian armed forces. International Human Right Watch argues that human rights violations only fuelled insurgency in most states. It is high time to ensure dignity of NE people and resolve AFSPA issue immediately.

Right now the separatist movements in Northeast have subsided but not died out. Most of these movments have devolved into criminal nexus that can be dealt with as a law and order problem. This is right time to push the path of development, representation and reconciliation to prevent another wave of separatism, assuming India is thinking forward about making a better nation. With corridors to both East Asia and South East Asia, India can build several business nodes in the Northeast and herald in an era of sustainable development in the region. I am not sure if there is political will and awareness at any level to make these changes but organized and informed people can do wonders.

Chapter 2. The Future Of Mobile Technology in India: Looking Beyond The Hype And Scandals

When we think of mobile communication there are a few images that flash in ones mind: one of the UPA (previous Indian government) telecommunication scandal, an image of people constantly talking on mobile phones and another of catchy advertisements inundating all forms of media. What gets hidden behind the curtain is the irreversible socioeconomic transformation of our society, hidden costs and benefits, changes in trade and foreign relations and most importantly the immense future possibilities. Here, we assess the road taken by the mobile sector till now, so that we can better shape the future. We ask if this technology can be the leading first sector where a currently non-existent dimension can be added to the Indian growth story; that of an innovation based economy.

First, let us look at the ways mobile technology has changed our lives. Primary service of the mobile technology, when initially introduced in 1999, was to provide voice communication but over the years, internet, mobile enterprise services, mobile-commerce and entertainment, are some of the services that have been added to the milieu. The reach of the mobile technology has changed accessibility and communication everywhere. Its use has spread in regions where the landline use is rather limited, for example even in a war-ravaged country of Afghanistan that has barely any landlines, 150,000 new cell phone subscribers are added every month. According to the telecom regulatory authority of India in October 2011, India had 600 million plus active wireless subscribers with around 65% subscription from urban areas. The evolution of wireless technology and the growth in data transfer rates has facilitated the spread of internet on mobile devices. With declining voice tariff, mobile operators have started providing entertainment services such as mobile music, mobile TV, mobile gaming, audios, videos and social networking etc. Mobile music that includes ring tone and song downloading is the most used service in India, primarily because of the urban youth use patterns. Rural sector usage is very utilitarian, with a whopping 40% of usage related to gathering agricultural information, while entertainment services are at a much lower 16%, and financial services such as mobile remittance and money at a healthy 8%, showing the pragmatic side of the country folks. This increased communication increases social mobility and are already proving to be a vehicle of social and economic transformation. In recent years, availability of services in various regional languages has made mobile services reachable to a bigger spectrum of people. To much chagrin of the political elites, mobile communication and internet have acted as a catalyst for social change too. The telecom industry currently directly contributes to more than 1.5% to the Indian GDP. When the tele-density saturates, then also for many years total usage will continue to increase, so this sector has immense potential for growth. More than 5 million jobs are created in India, directly or indirectly due to the telecom sector and this is expected to increase to 12 million soon but this is an underestimate of the true social and economic impact. This is the first time for many in the remote regions to know about supply and demand dynamics of their business on everyday basis and being able to talk to end user of their product. Urban migrant workers and troops stationed in remote regions can get in touch with their family on a regular basis now and financial transactions can be conducted at ones fingertips, bypassing the long queues and the customary bribing of the clerical staff. This transformation and mass empowerment is reflected by the fact that currently 1% growth in tele-density results in a 3% increase in the rate of GDP growth. Given such an important role of mobile sector in developing world, one can consider it a basic utility and should be vary of not repeating mistakes of US of letting some unaccounted monopolies develop in this sector.

Wait a minute; let me not make you feel that there are way too many rainbows in this sunny story of mobile revolution. There are dark sides of the mobile sector; some, where light can reach easily and some that would need novel solutions. These are two dimensions of negatives of this mobile revolution in India: one the negative impact of the mobile technology itself and the other where Indian society is specifically lagging behind in gaining from this transformation. In India, one undergoes an unabated harassment of unsolicited calls, texts, pop ups, and gets enrolled in unwanted services without ones consent. Even though National Do Not Call Registry has been set up to curb unsolicited calls and there is now a daily limit of sending 200 SMSs per number, spammers and sales people seem to be outpacing sluggish control measures. Indians are also yet to catch up with the global usage for smarter monitoring of constantly evolving situations like stock markets and developing news stories of their concern. Mobile commerce has enabled increasing number of Indians to do their money transaction in a secured manner using mobile technology, including buying or selling goods, financial services like accessing bank accounts, booking tickets, paying bills and stock trading but the segment using these services from mobile is somewhat limited due to unfamiliarity with the services and also due to security concerns. Bandwidth insufficiency and unreliable network connectivity are the limitations that cause security concerns in India. Mobile technology has a potential in healthcare and education but that potential remains largely untapped at present. Mobile usage and Internet in general have changed the work habits for some people in negative ways and usage of mobile sets during driving has increased traffic accidents. Fixing the behavior of public and cops, who violate traffic laws alike, is an easier fix than the attention related issues and Internet addiction. The use of current technology of batteries in mobile devices is a concern world over due to limited charge storage issues and dependence on rare earth metals from other countries for their manufacture. India suffers from a lack of proper disposal of mobile parts in an environmentally sound manner, although higher second hand usage of instrument reduces the total environmental footprint.

Apart from the above-mentioned problems, there are some issues that are closest to our hearts. Despite 600 million plus users in India, double the size of total American population, leave innovation, even manufacture sector thrives mostly on compiling products manufactured elsewhere, instead of significant domestic production. This lack of high tech production and innovation is not unique to the mobile sector but a general plague afflicting India. Apart from the drawbacks of the industry that need fixing, the failure to innovate is in a bigger part a result of failure of the academic and the governmental research institutions. In US, Europe, Japan and South Korea, fundamentals of novel technologies are born either in the research universities or in the governmental institutions. Indian government and academic settings, especially ones located near centers of power, like the University of Delhi, a darkest example of what is rotten in Indian research, are a swamp for the talented to perish and a bottomless pit for sucking taxpayer's money. These universities with departments conducting research, have politically appointed cronies in the positions of vice chancellor, dean of research, and heads of departments, people that have no single internationally known academic achievement or mentionable success in translating an idea to a commercially viable product. These small men who cast long shadows, meddle with research, play political games and harass academics to maintain their positions are frequently guilty of prolonging failed mega projects to fatten their chauffeurs. A vibrant industry and academia interaction is the backbone of an innovation-based economy and for such a healthy interaction to occur in India, a transparent process of depoliticizing academia and government run research initiatives is direly needed. We hope more Indians, whether in India or abroad would see this bad situation as a challenge and an opportunity, as we do, to lead innovation though efforts in basic research and industry. The business sector also needs visionaries and business leaders who can enable innovation by choosing to invest in the right people to do the right projects, more so in the times when there exists not much of a respectable academic research apparatus. Given that India has one of the largest mobile markets in the world, the mobile sector has a very large potential for India's development.

Chapter 3. A Case Against Big Fat Indian Weddings

Indians like weddings. Big ones: with all the pomp and show. These occasions there are blessed by the presence of third and fourth degree, almost unrelated relatives and friends of friends of friends. From Indian standards, you are made aware that you are not doing that well in life if half your town is not present at your wedding. The matches made in heaven are also no less interesting than the festivities. These matches tend to be made by Auntijis (reference to all women older than you by 5 to 10 years, something unpalatable to me but reality of India), matrimonial websites, love-arranged marriages, arranged-love marriages and once in a while by people being stupid enough to actually fall in love.

While these moments to remember can be made more personal or traditional or both, at a lot less expense, somehow investing in house, gold and big fat weddings is a national obsession. People take loans to pay for the arrangements and then there is a Stone Age custom of dowry. Even wedding invitations come with gifts and dry fruits these days. Guests at wedding have to shell out expensive gifts or cash as well, that tends to be compared after the event, to judge the affection of benefactor to the couple. It is basically a big fat event where everyone loses a lot of money. One can keep on writing more scathing critique of big fat weddings or even try to defend some of the good parts of this over-bloated new tradition but I am only interested in making a pragmatic and patriotic argument against excessive materialism.

While there is enough money in with middle class and upwards in the country very little of it gets spent on things that should matter. A large amount is spent on pomp and show. Why is that we are so averse to investing back in the economy and growing our own personal fortunes? The distant relatives that one usually never meets or cares about can anyway happily go about their business, without having to attend few more mandatory weddings.

If you think money is to spend and to hell with future investments, then too why spend it on feeding the well-fed? Why have a pretentious large affair? Make the spending count. Take a longer break than a touristy honeymoon. Go explore the world or for that matter, India. How many non-touristy destinations in India you have spent a week at? If you are conscientious how about opening a school or doing something for street kids or health care for poor? I can write several more suggestions but I am sure you can think of what matters to you. Anyway I need to stop writing, as I need to come up with a good excuse or an argument with my parents, who want to drag me to a big fat wedding in few hours and convince me that my India visit can be best utilized if they get to arrange a fat one for me too.

Chapter 4. Glitter is not all that good

India is the largest consumer of gold in the world. Not just now but in Athenian councils and Roman senates, a vexing issue used to be the loss of gold coins to India in trade. In fact, now we know that most of gold in both Gupta and Kushana period (that resulted in some Indophiles calling India as the "Golden Bird") was of Mediterranean origin.

Now that gold is not tied to coinage and currency cost in any way, why is that still today more than 700 kgs of gold is smuggled in India every day? Indians like glitter, bling bling, pomp and well, maybe bit of a safe investment. I am not going to argue against the shine of gold, as I do not think my writing will dissuade those who are goldstruck because of its glitter, but I would like to question the sagacity of gold as a good investment for personal and national economic growth.

First let me ask the smaller question – Is gold all that promising for personal economic growth? Between 2011 to now, there has been a 30% decline in its price and more so in this day and age when there are so many better investment options, then why go for gold? But for the sake of argument, let us say that gold is a safe and good investment for you as a person but here is the big question – Is gold good for the country? Gold or for that matter anything that takes capital out of circulation from the economy is slowing down India's economic engine. Gold is the kind of investment that does not result in the size of economy to grow. It takes out much needed capital, does not generate jobs and most importantly it does not open new avenues for future growth. We need productive investment back in the society. Gold is simply not in the national interest of India.

Affluent Indians need to explore the Wild West frontiers instead of sitting in the comfort of their homes on piles of gold. The modern equivalent of Wild West frontiers is exploring new ventures in economic and social entrepreneurship. Dynamism instead of the love of glitter put West on the map and is behind the rise of the China in the East. It is time for the elephant of Indian economy to wake up from its sleep, shrug of its heavy golden ornaments and take off.

Chapter 5. Ensuring a strong currency

I am writing about Indian rupee but this can be of relevance to any currency. Stable exchange rates are much needed for stable global economy.

What makes Rupee's Dollar value oscillate every full moon night or anytime when you look at the Rupee wrong? Is it that the Indian economy fluctuates so very rapidly? Or is it that the Reserve Bank of India (RBI) suddenly decides to change the total currency in circulation. Neither Indian economy nor RBI's fiscal policies exhibit the kind of epileptic seizures needed to match the fits in the exchange value.

Despite significantly higher growth rate of Indian economy than the US in the last three decades Rupee has weakened to half its value (to the current rates above Rs 60 for 1 USD). Indian inflation, although much higher than US, even when compounded in the equation, is still insufficient to account for the rates. While it would not be fair to compare the exact exchange rate of 1966, where Rs. 7.5 was equal to one USD, because the rate was pegged by the government and not by market and the total Indian currency in circulation was insignificant compared to now, but it still serves as a good indicator of the overall downward spiral over the years.

This begs three important questions: What are the reasons for very high exchange rates and extreme fluctuations? More importantly, what impact exchange rates have on the Indian economy?

Reasons for high exchange rates and fluctuations in prices. Flow of dollars can be and is actually used to regulate the exchange rate. It does not mean that US Federal Reserve actions are to be blamed for each or even most fluctuations. There are many international banking conglomerates that regulate the international cash flow more than the not so federally controlled, US Federal Reserve. There is also an additional economic dimension that anyone's classical training in the tradition of Adam Smith or Marx ill prepares for. Let us do a thought experiment. Say, US prints twice the amount of currency off a sudden but if the faith in US economy remains strong enough that inflation is not 100% but only 20% then US could grow its Dollar economy (not the whole economy) artificially by 80%. I am exaggerating the total potential of such expansion to illustrate a point that if a dominant economy chooses it can simply mint more money. Not all the US Federal Reserve and several international banking conglomerates' actions are synergistic, so one should not view those influences as monolithic. Speculation market and the scope of influence of speculators on the exchange rate is a gray area. A flip side of the coin to high dollar value, is that given India does almost all its trade in dollar, a sudden decline in dollar value can send catastrophic news to Indian interests. So India has to rely on the peace and prosperity of US and hope it does not start another all consuming war with some country that might actually matter.

Impact of exchange rate on Indian economy. From India's lentils, fossil fuels to its several high tech purchases, several key supplies come from the global market. Any fluctuation in the dollar exchange rate can send shiver up the spine of Indian economy.

Chapter 6. Quest For India's Sustainable Development

Development is much needed in a country that has the 3rd of the world's poorest people. While development is talked about as a buzzword, the models of development do not get discussed enough. India needs a sustainable approach to development.

Ecologically sustainable development

Ecological sustainability is a must for both ethical and pragmatic reasons. We have no moral right to end billions of years of evolution in few short centuries. India is currently a land of open litter, with toxins seeping in soil at unprecedented rates. It would take several thousands of years to clear these toxins out of the ecosystem under normal cycling. Due to the need and greed of land mafia, vast swathes of agricultural land are irreversibly being transformed into construction space.

Pesticide and fertilizer use in our agricultural sector is currently uncontrolled. While carbon emissions are now being controlled but many toxic fumes continue to be released in environment. The Special Economic Zones are currently Special Eco-disaster Zones that are just simmering Bhopals, waiting to explode. There is a dire need to make industrial growth ecologically sustainable. Environmental regulation does not mean bowing down to the whims of West that would like to maintain its dominance at all costs. Regulations and their enforcement need to evolve from Indian demands, constraints and environmental vision and ethics. In addition to governmental efforts, citizen's ownership of their country is a must. A single look at Indian cities shows a stark contrast between the insides of people's houses and outside. In the land of litter the inside of houses are impeccably clean while outside can at times be just a dignified toilet.

There are several issues that are completely missing from the mainstream national discourse such as deforestation, one of the world's lowest ground water tables and extreme underutilization of plentiful renewable energy resources. While the most systematic deforestation happened on the orders of Pant, who let anyone and everyone clear as much of Tarai region after the partition but this carnage has not stopped even in the present age of environment consciousness. There are several countries with much higher population densities than India that have managed to keep much higher fraction of land dedicated to forests than India. A first and immediately actionable step to manage deforestation is to ensure that subsistence agriculture is stopped and a quick transition is made to sustainable higher crop yields. A lack of information and proper resources also translates into one of the highest pest related losses (exceeding Rs 50,000 crores in worth annually), despite very high use of pesticides in several parts of the country. The losses of crops after harvesting are also one of the highest in the world. Improvements in these obvious sectors would reduce the burden on our fragile ecosystem and forests.

We need to step out of the mold of doctrinal support or opposition to any approach or live in the world of black and whites, especially on the hot-button issues of GM crops and organic farming. More evidence-based policymaking that centers on people and sustainability is immediately needed.

Social and Economic Sustainability

Capitalism is a mixed story, just as are so many other nineteenth and twentieth century constructs. The success side of the coin of capitalism has relied in part on individual entrepreneurship and innovation, just as much it has relied on the availability of fair or unfair surplus capital. Even if one has a doctrinal view of infallibility of capitalism, one must wake up to the fact that 99% of people are not able to get above daily grind, such that even brains smarter than that of Steve Jobs would be only making ends meet. The disparity in India is hindering the use of full potential of Indian population. This is compounded by the further stratification of society due to caste and community barriers.

Harnessing the true potential of India is not possible as long as we stay in the grips of crony capitalism. Crony capitalism has resulted in not just an economic strangling of the society and displacement of several people but also in grave harm to our environment and cultural heritage. In Karnataka, now even one of the best Vijayanagara ruins at Hampi have started paying the price of uncontrolled mining. It is not just the lower strata that suffers due to crony capitalism but also entrepreneurs interested in honest innovative business who are afraid of nepotism, red tape and corruption. In addition to reducing corruption, the economy also needs to move more towards end product high-tech economy. Government needs to evolve mechanisms that value equally the intellectual capital as the financial capital that is needed to transform the economy.

Steps are needed to reduce the barriers of entry in high tech sectors. This would also eliminate monopolies and evolve a more technologically advanced economy. While it is important to ensure the safety net and Indian assertion, one must not take an isolationist position in the world. One must understand just as we must not repeat mistakes of capitalism, we should also learn from mistakes of other experiments. Instead of a doctrinal approach the approach needs to be for the benefit of everyone, with the weakest section being our first concern. Instead of short-term relief mechanisms, we must establish long-term largely self-sustaining mechanisms that ensure upward mobility and safety net for masses.

One must also remember that trickle down does not work. Pulling up of large sections of society cannot be exclusivist, castist and nepotistic. In India there is another social construct of caste that reduces social mobility. Unfortunately a change in that will take public awareness and not just political changes. It remains to be seen if anyone would be up to this biggest task of catalyzing such a change even few years down the lane.

Chapter 7. Need to regularize contractual labor

There have been several strokes of pen by the legislature that have left an indelible mark on our society. Right to education, land reforms, right to information and many such legislative acts also happen to be political masterstrokes for those who stand or accidentally land on the right side of history. CPM's single act of somewhat genuine land reforms in West Bengal gave them several decades of unquestioned support from the countryside as it empowered previously landless millions. A whole generation that benefitted from that state level change turned blind eye to CPM's several colossal failures because of what this single act of land reform had done to empower their families.

Dealing with the widespread menace of contractual jobs is a dire need. A legislative change about it has the potential of influencing all walks of Indian life at a much larger scale than land reforms and enable India to be a more equitable, more just and happier country. It is a surprise that neither the opportunists nor the idealists of Indian politics have taken up this issue seriously.

Contractual jobs are only a necessity where the job is of a small scale and the demand for employment is temporary. In India, most contractual jobs do not meet these criteria but account for one of the largest chunks of the national employment figures. The reality of contractual job is that if the monthly salary is 10,000 Rupees then the private sector employer pays 3000 Rupees and asks the contractual employee to sign for 10,000 Rupees. In a lower end job, there is not much that the poor worker can do, as a protest would mean the termination of employment. This fate of contractual jobs is not limited to daily wage earners and the lowest rung of Indian society but there are educated middle class people, such as schoolteachers across India signing for much higher salaries than they receive. In the absence of a "free market", with the specific situation of "jobs exceeding labor supply", a contractual worker is always left at the mercy of employer's exploitation. The employees have to work unpaid hours and do tasks that are not part of the original job description. Contractual nature of jobs largely precludes work force from participating in trade unions and receive other benefits of permanent workers, such as retirement plans and sick leaves.

This exploitative situation is not limited to the private sector. These days both central and state governments hire people mostly on contractual basis for jobs that are in reality permanent in nature. For example, Delhi Transport Corporation hires contractual employees and then throws them out of job every few months, sending them to the back of the line, so it does not have to offer permanent employment and its associated benefits. Overwhelming majority of Indian society does not have any old age and disability security because of being on a contractual job. It forces large section of work force and their families to face uncertain future, everyday harassment and bleak future prospects. Doing away with the menace of contractual jobs would usher in a new era of social, economic and geographical mobility needed to transform India into a developed country.

I would hope for legislative changes to ensure that contractual jobs are offered in India, if and only if the strict criteria for it are met. I would also urge towards working on the actual distribution of signed pay, where contractual job criteria are met, with specific legislation to ensure strict punishment for violators.

About Sukant Khurana

Dr. Sukant Khurana is a scientist, artist, writer, and entrepreneur. He was born in Delhi, India and has spent most of his professional career in United States. His science focuses on understanding functioning of brain, ameliorating human suffering through technology development, and data science, while his art focuses on exploring the human condition. Sukant has worked on efforts to encourage education, sustainable development, women empowerment, environmental, and healthcare issues. In free time, Sukant can be found working on various art projects, traveling off beat paths, capturing wildlife on his camera or having long chats with friends over a cup of coffee.

Photocredit: Costance Burkin

Connect with Sukant Khurana

Facebook author and artist pages:
https://www.facebook.com/SukantKhuranaauthorsite;
https://www.facebook.com/Sukant-1625360857788363/
Follow me on Twitter: https://twitter.com/sukant_khurana
Connect on LinkedIn: http://www.linkedin.com/pub/sukant-khurana/43/a23/755
Visit my websites:
http://www.brainnart.com
http://www.dataisnotjustdata.com

www.ingramcontent.com/pod-product-compliance
Lightning Source LLC
Chambersburg PA
CBHW072023290526
45787CB00014B/1764